PLEASURATION I

By

Kelvin Brown

ISBN: 978-0-7596-3604-0 (sc)
ISBN:978-0-7596-3603-3 (e)

1stBooks – rev. 08/8/01

Pleasuration is giving love and devotion to your mate, to the extent that there,

Is no need for any intimate feelings, outside of your relationship.

Pleasuration is being spontaneous in areas, in which you haven't been,

Pleasuration is growing, sharing, caring, for your special love.

Plesuration is sacrificing some of life's little pleasures to make sure that,

Your mate has had her needs met.

Pleasuration is sometimes imaging what it would be like without your mates.

Then knowing that, going to your mate and reassuring him/her that you really, truly care.

But, most of all....

Pleasuration is what you believe what it takes to fulfill your mates needs and wants.

Working to be the greatest love that you can be to one true love.

TABLE OF CONTENTS

IF YOU COULD LEARN (TO LOVE ME)

If you could learn to love me,
My life would be so grand,
With so much joy and ecstasy,
With your hand in my hand.

If you would learn to love me,
Our love would be so unique,
It would stretch as wide as the sea,
And deeper that beneath.

If you try to learn to love me,
Just as long as there's a start,
I'll be the man you want me to be,
By loving with soul and heart.

If undecided, if you should love me,
Take your time….let the thought sink in,
I'll be waiting so patiently,
For that hopeful moment to begin.

If you don't think that you could love me,

Because there's something that I lack,

Then I'll simply set your love free….

By kindly stepping back.

THREE WISHES

If I could have three wishes,
I'd want for nothing more,
First I'd like to be granted your kisses,
Which raise me from the floor.

They're soft and sweet so sensuous,
I love each single touch,
I could never ever get enough,
Your kisses mean so much.

Secondly, I want to be,
The man you'd love for life,
And I'd love you oh so tenderly,
From morning through the night.

I'd give you all the love you'd need,
I'd wrap my love around you,
You wouldn't have to beg or plead,
That's what I'm here to do.

Last but not least, we'd be as one,

In mind, spirit and soul,

Knowing and growing in the warmth of the sun,

Caring and sharing when it's cold.

I'd promise to love you through all my days,

Treating you like the true lady you are,

Pleasing you in so many various ways,

Because you'd be my shining star.

If I can't have my wishes granted,

I'd make sure that one would come true,

I'd pursue the way I planned it,

And spend my life loving you.

<u>YOUR LOVE IN ME</u>

In my eyes,

No other woman possesses the

Beauty that you show,

In my eyes,

If there is,

I don't even want to know.

In my eyes,

You're as pretty as a flower,

And in my eyes,

You get lovelier with each hour.

In my arms,

Makes me feel like a King,

In my arms,

I'd do my everything.

In my arms,

You fit just like a glove;

And in my arms,

I feel a glowing Love.

5

In my Heart,

I feel a pounding strong,

In my Heart,

It lasts so ever long.

In my Heart,

I've a need to share,

In my Heart,

I will always keep you there.

In my mind,

You are the one I need,

In my mind,

You are a part of me.

In my mind,

You are, the only Lover,

And in my mind,

Above and under the cover.

In my soul,

I feel peace and tranquility,

In my Soul,

In part, because you're near to me.

In my Soul,

I no longer have to search for more,

In my soul,

You have opened up that door.

In my Love,

There is plain and simple truth,

In my Love

Baby, I've found you.

And in my Love,

There's room for you always,

In my Love,

Whatever come what may.

In my eyes, my arms, my heart,

I hope that we won't part,

In my mind, my Soul, my Love,

We have the best Love that ever was.

LOVE'S IN WAITING

I remember that moment we first kissed,
I hoped and wished time would be still,
And today your sweet lips are missed,
I haven't changed in the way I feel.

Something is there and I could tell,
By the feelings I got from each touch,
Along with a bit of a dizzy spell,
I want your love so much.

I want your love to be all mine,
As long as there's a day and night,
Forever growing till the end of time,
Reaching higher than a bird in flight.

Let me be the one to love you strong,

Share your love make real my dream,

Replace my hunger with the fruit I long,

And my love will flow like an endless stream.

Open up your heart, just try,

I mean every word my lips say,

And if you feel half as much as I,

Then baby we're on our way.

Don't pass me by, no not, again!

Don't leave me here on the shelf,

I want to share your joy and pain,

Give you love like no one else.

It's been a while since I kissed your lips,

Been some time since I've seen your face,

But I consistently think of what could exist,

Having your love fill this empty space.

I want you to know that I love you so much,

And I want you for the rest of my days,

Caring and sharing and loving tough,

To please you in so many ways.

I'll keep counting my blessings in the night,

And continuously wishing upon a star,

I'll wait until you think it's right,

To let me be where you are.

But don't make me wait a lifetime,

Wishing my days and nights through,

It's better when they're yours and mine,

Life is more fun done with two.

Just say that you will, sweetest one,

Say that you'll give it a try,

There's no one here under the sun,

Who could love you better than I.

11

MY LOVER

I looked into the eyes of my lover,

Standing there toe to toe,

I could see there was another,

And I knew that I had to go.

Then I felt the heart of my lover,

I could feel deep down within,

There'd be no more under the cover,

And at most, we'd just be friends.

So I kissed the lips of my lover,

To make this brief session complete,

For I knew there wasn't another,

Who possessed a kiss so sweet.

Then I held my lover in my arms,

So tight the coldness came through,

Her love had expired along with her charms,

And everything else was past due.

Then I held the hand of my use to be,

With an absence of tears on her face,

And can't seem to understand why she,

Thought that I needed to be replaced.

Then I lost the sight of my lover,

Of which I had become to know,

Prayers can't help me from above,

To change a heart that wouldn't grow.

At last I some how realized,

Though it took awhile to see,

After the tears dried from my eyes,

It was best I let it be.

Kelvin Brown

Of all the hurt, the sorrow, the pain,

The good times, the bad and such,

Now I'm ready to love again,

But this time twice as much.

There's a lady out there in need you see,

I am absolutely sure of that,

Who wants to be loved tenderly,

No bull, no brag just fact.

I know that I'm one of the best,

When it comes to satisfying,

So if you're good, then I suggest,

That you get busy trying.

"THE THOUGHT OF YOU"

The thought of you is a partial gift,

Just a section of what you possess,

It's there to give me that special lift,

Until your're held in my firm carress.

It merely makes my life complete,

Like nobody or nothing can,

And I'm so happy that life's so sweet,

I'm so glad that I'm your chosen man.

The thought of you is a ray of Sun,

It's the brightest star in the night,

When you're not here it keeps me warm,

'Cause you're missed when out of sight.

The thought of you, is a feeling so nice,

There's none, that can compare,

Without a doubt, no need to think twice,

You're the reason that I care.

The thought of you makes me feel,

There's no mountain I can't climb,

But…there's no feeling like when you're near to me,

When each moment's like the first time.

The thought of you is knowing,

I've got someone to love,

And, it just keeps on growing,

Reaching for the skies above.

The thought of you is a gentle touch,

Soft as a surgeon's cotton,

A touch that means so very much,

One that's never, ever forgotten.

The thought of you is a piercing pain,

That's comforted by your smile,

Like the cooling of a gentle rain,

When it's been hot a while.

The thought of you is always there,

Whenever I need a friend,

You give me love, I show I care,

Until the very end.

The thought of you cannot be measured,

Although I feel it's worth,

You're sweet Love right here is treasured,

More than anything on earth.

I will always keep the thought of you,

Deep in the pit of my heart,

Like I promised you I'd do,

Right from the very start.

17

AT THIS LEVEL OF LOVE

At this level of Love,

I needn't get any higher,

Already I'm way above,

The heat from any fire.

I'm so completely satisfied,

Now that I have you,

And as long as you're by my side,

There's no limit to what I can do.

Your Love took so long to find,

And now I'm going to do it right,

Every morning, every night, every time,

I'll Love you with all my might.

At this level of Love,

I know just where I stand,

Fitted together like a hand in glove,

I am one very happy man.

I want you to feel just as I do,

Then I'm sure we'll be together,

It's better than a dream come true,

Living and Loving forever and ever.

You give me the feeling, I've so longed for,

And I need you here with me,

I want to Love you more and more,

This was always meant to be.

At this Level of Love,

It just couldn't get any better,

Everynight I thank the stars above,

For finally bringing us together.

Your smile is captured in my mind,

And our heart beats are synchronized,

I know and you know it's right this time,

My life's been energized.

I'm smiling, I'm styling with grace,

I'm hailing, I'm sailing world on top,

I've got a woman with a lovely face,

And with a body that, just won't stop.

At this level of Love,

I'm at the Zenith of my stride,

I'm so satisfied with your kiss and hug,

Overwhelmed to have you by my side.

All I ask, is that you never tire,

Of this love I'm giving you,

And I'll keep on feeding this fire,

So hot, so sizzling, and so true.

<u>"NATURAL LOVE"</u>

As I woke at the break of dawn,

And the sun's rays touched my face,

I needed you to keep me warm,

For there's none can take your place.

The birds were singing a melody,

As it filled this heart of mine,

They must have been singing for you and me,

Cause it made me feel so fine.

The winds were flowing through the trees,

As the leaves danced gentle and free,

Up and down to the side with ease,

As if they knew the beat.

The skies had opened up their arms,

To let the sunshine through,

Which made me long for your sweet charms,

Girl…I'm so in love with you.

With so many lovely things there are,

It's hard not to think of your Love,

Cause you are my morning and evening Star,

You're my angel from up above.

Being near you, I'm a mountain high,

I'm an eagle with soaring wings,

And for you I'd touch the sky,

To give you love lasting.

I…so much enjoy your all and all,

I'm fascinated by someone so sweet,

And I sit impatient for your call,

Oh, how you do what you do to me.

Just let me soak in your sweet touch,

Let me bathe in your after glow,

Nothing in this world could mean so much,

When you say that you love me so.

I'll love you until the day before ever,

And nurture this love til the end,

That's how long we'll be together,

So of this Love, you can depend.

"FOR DEAR MERCY"

I've cherished every moment we've spent together,

My Heart will forever hold a part,

Of that Joy you shared, as if forever,

I've Loved you from the start.

Even now I feel my heart beats stronger,

Whenever, wherever I think of you,

And I try to hold on longer,

Than you really want me to.

You are a very Special Love,

Who brightens up my whole life and beyond,

You'll always be the one that I dream of,

When it's all been said and done.

And if there is no possibility,

That I can't have you all,

I will be there Special "DE",

The moment that you call.

You've said that I don't need you,

But I must and just disagree,

There's nothing that I wouldn't do,

Just to have you next to me.

I wonder do you really miss me,

When I haven't seen you for a while,

Then wish that you could kiss me,

So I could see your smile.

And when I think I've lost you,

And you no longer care,

The only thing that I can do,

Is dream, and you are there.

The only thing that beats a dream,

Is having you right here,

Where I can "show you" what I mean,

Then tell you "I Love you" dear.

Right now I miss your Lovin' so much,

But I can hold on fast,

I can still feel your tender touch,

Because that's how long it lasts.

Sometimes I want your Love so bad,

It seems like I can taste it,

And knowing of the good times we've had,

It seems a crime to waste it.

Don't take away the only thing,

That I have come to know,

And leave me just remembering,

Just how much I Love you so.

Let me fill your heart with Joy and Laughter,

Let me show you how I feel,

The day before and that day after,

Don't deny when love is real.

Let me be the one you talk to,

Let me share your ups and downs,

I'll sacrifice my All for you,

For You, I'll always be around.

So I hope this Love won't be forgot,

Like the feather in the wind,

My Love for you will never stop,

Until the very end.

SWEET AND CLEAR

To me you're like sweet music,

Everytime you're almost near,

And unknowingly you use it,

Because it comes in soft and clear.

You're so captivating no imitating,

Like a rhapsody in blue,

My heart skips a beat while awaiting,

To hear a familiar tune.

You're like a Sunday morning serenade,

While birds in the background sing,

Sounds so good when its been played,

And with joy to the heart you bring.

Vibrations from my head to feet,

A slight tremble in my finger tips,

Everlasting rhythm not ever complete,

Coming from your tender lips.

The vibes I receive pick up the sound,

That no one else has ever heard,

Everytime that you're around,

And without you saying a word.

A melody to make my mood,

Which takes me through the day,

A positive mental attitude,

On the thought of the music you create.

It's everywhere, I hear it there,

So soothing to the ear,

Sometimes people stop and stare,

But it's not for them to hear.

It plays for me and not for those,

Who don't reserve the time,

And I'm so glad that you compose,

Each and every line.

You're Bach, Beethoven, a symphony,

An orchestration that's equal to none,

You're sweet joy, you're harmony,

Being done like it's never been done.

So play for me a melody,

From the music that you bring,

And I will keep them secretly,

In the heart that loves to sing.

DREAMS AND THINGS

I dream of kisses tenderly,
I've memorized their feel,
Sometimes you get so next to me,
At times I think they are real.

I dream of those tomorrows,
And a Love that's in full bloom;
I don't have time for sorrows,
Because there isn't any room.

I dream of how to Love you,
And hope you'll understand;
Do the things you want to do,
For my heart is your's to command.

I dream of being by your side,

At that moment you awaken;

And knowing you were satisfied,

After your Love's been taken.

I dream of countless hours,

That I'm away from you,

But your Love has the powers,

To turn my gray skies blue.

I dream of holding you so tight,

No one could tear us apart;

And if by chance that it's done right,

You'll only hear one heart.

I've dreamed of you in most my dreams,

Your love and Precious Charms,

then those dreams don't mean a thing,

Til I have you in my arms.

So when I feel I've dreamt enough,

And my nights are through;

Just simply stay in Love with me

Cause…

I'm so in Love with you!

<u>LOVELY LADY</u>

You're a very beautiful Lady,
I've passed you a many time,
I'm not the only one that goes crazy,
It's not your fault, you're fine.

I'm not trying to distract you,
Or in any case get fresh,
But you look so great and so smooth,
You stand out from the rest.

I know you've heard it all before,
It's something you already know,
So I'm not trying to be a bore,
When I say you've got a glow.

I've wondered if your personality,
Is as pleasant as your smile?
If it is then I must agree,
That you've got a beautiful style.

So sweet, unique the smile you wear,

That's never out of place,

There's luxurious hair soft as the air,

To highlight your lovely face.

I've never had the chance to meet,

Someone as fair as you,

You could make a man's life sweet,

Or make his dreams come true.

But I'm a guy who just can't help,

Saying just the way I feel,

When beauty is in someone else,

And I can see it's real.

Oh, I could write about you,

And complete my poetry books,

Then have enough for a Part 2,

About your mind as well as looks.

Kelvin Brown

I do hope you're not offended,

By my somewhat carried away rhymes,

For it's certainly not intended,

Seems I can't help myself at times.

"A SPECIAL VALENTINE"

Happy Valentine's Day to you my Love,
I give my heart to you,
Cause you are the one I'm always thinking of,
And I hope you feel that way too!

There's cards and gifts that I could give,
But there's none made specially,
So for the moment our Love lives,
I'll write from the heart of me.

I'm really into loving you,
No one could need you more,
The thought of you, just brings me through,
It's deep down to the core.

There's no place I'd rather be,
Than right there by your side,
Me loving you, You loving me,
It's hard for us to hide.

37

Please bear with me, a time will be,

That we will be together,

And build a Love so strong so sweet,

The kind that lasts forever.

So here's to you, my Sweet Valentine,

Please hear me when I say,

I have got to make you mine,

At least, forever and a day.

And if by chance or circumstance,

It seems it's taking longer,

It only means that this romance,

Is gonna be much stronger.

Well, I won't simply waste your time,

No longer than I should,

Just be my only Valentine,

And I'll try to be Damm good!

BEAUTIFUL WONDER

Chilled soft rain drops kissing her face,
Only to be warmed by her sweet smile,
Dressed in her simple but soft pink lace,
In the nude she'd still have style.

She's in Love with those simple things,
Just to smell a fresh flower is a ghast,
The sound of a church bell when it rings,
And she'll listen as long as it lasts.

She's in love with all and all,
Guess that's why her beauty shows,
She's lifted she's gifted through summer and fall,
She's happy no matter which way the wind blows.

She's fascination and anticipation,
She's full of joy and sweet song,
She is beauty a lovely creation,
Complimented by a heart that's strong.

As the snow flakes touch her hair,

As they gently lay upon it,

They seem to make a display so rare,

Which resembles a woven bonnet.

Her lovely flowers have all gone to sleep,

For they rest for springtime once more,

When again they'll rise from underneath,

More beautiful than ever before.

Now she'll feed the birds an other creatures,

Who feel her warmth and come near,

There's rabbits and squirrels with different features,

She speaks softly and settled and clear.

Her face is blushed by the new fallen snow,

And the sun has vanished from sight,

Where will she go, guess I'll never know,

As she enters into the night.

The following day, she's right there,

Exciting refreshing and new,

She doesn't know how much I care,

And there's nothing I wouldn't do.

I'd like to one day know the love,

Which she is always giving,

To feel, to touch her world above,

Her undying spirit for living.

I won't disturb her peace and tranquility,

My joy is just watching her play,

Even though she may never see me,

I love her more and more each day.

<u>ANGEL LOVE</u>

EARTHBOUND ANGEL HEAVEN'S DELIGHT,
I NEED YOUR LOVE ALL THROUGH THE NIGHT,
I REACH TO TOUCH, BUT YOU'RE NOT THERE,
THE SCENT OF PERFUME IN THE AIR.

THOSE VISIONS OF YOU RUN THROUGH MY HEAD,
BUT I'D RATHER HAVE YOU INSTEAD,
SO I CAN HEAR YOUR WARM HEART BEAT,
THAT MAGIC MOMENT, THAT OUR LIPS MEET.

A LOVE LIKE THIS IS NOT A MISTAKE,
IT'S BROUGHT TOGETHER BY THE HANDS OF FATE,
HOT AND SIZZLING LIKE A FIRE,
NEVER COOLING, JUST CLIMBING HIGHER.

AND IF LOVE IS BLIND, THEN I CAN' SEE,
ONLY YOU LYING HERE NEXT TO ME;
WANTING YOU MORE THAN YOU'LL EVER KNOW,
LIL SEXY WOMAN I MISS YOU SO.

PRECIOUS TIME'S NOT OUR'S TO WASTE,

WHEN WE MAKE LOVE FACE TO FACE,

EVERY SECOND IT GROWS STRONGER,

DUE TO ABSENCE OUR HEARTS GROW FONDER.

SO KISS ME LOVE, HOLD ME TIGHT,

ALTHOUGH IT'S ONLY FOR ONE NIGHT;

LET'S JUST MAKE THIS MOMENT LAST,

YOUR SWEET LOVE IS ALL I HAVE.

ONE DAY SOON WE'LL BE TOGETHER,

I HOPE YOU'LL LEAVE ME NEVER,

SO MY LOVE, BE MY LIFE,

I WILL ALWAYS TREAT YOU RIGHT.

<u>NEEDING YOU</u>

All I can do is dream about you,
The moment I close my eyes,
But oh how it hits me when I come to,
You're not there then I realize.

There's a picture of you in my mind,
A touch of your smile in my heart,
I'll always remember time after time,
For we are soon to depart.

Heaven knows what I feel is real,
An undying love with a passion,
Don't you know it would be a thrill,
To share your love is all I'm asking.

Deep down in my heart, I'm for sure,
And there is no doubt in my mind,
For my ailment you are the cure,
So Love me till the end of time.

I need love, but only yours will do,

And my arms are opened wide,

If you don't believe what I say is true,

Into my heart, won't you look inside.

<u>UNINTENTIONAL LOVE</u>

So you love me now,

Then why's it so sad?

I still can't believe how,

I could Love anybody this bad.

But you know you're that special thing,

That's happened to my life,

And with that magical joy you bring,

Even makes my darkest days bright.

Sometimes I wish we'd never met,

Cause any day you may be gone,

One things for sure I won't forget,

Your love that was oh so strong.

At times I wish I'd saw you first,

Or at another point in time,

I need your Love to quench my thirst,

With those lips as sweet as wine.

Everytime I think of you,

Which is every night and day,

I wish for one dream to come true,

And that is that you'll stay.

I heard a song not long ago,

"If you Love someone set them free",

so if that's true and I Love you so,

Then I'll have to let you be.

I've never Loved like this before,

And I probably won't again,

Right now I want you more and more,

O Love you're the living end.

I just can't help the way I feel,

You're a one in a Lifetime Love,

It feels like a dream but it's for real,

Just like the stars above.

I hate to think how it would be,

If we were out of touch,

No more talking passionately,

I'm already missing you so very much.

I won't give up, not easily,

I love you so my Dear,

Even in my dreams you'll be with me,

As for my heart you'll always be near.

But in this time, day and age,

Finances, Romances and such,

We'll just have to turn the page,

Just remember to keep in touch.

<u>MYSTIC LOVE</u>

I took a double take when I saw her face,

Amazed somewhat dazed at the view,

I felt at ease and not out of place,

And there, yes there was you.

At first (I thought) no don't say a word,

She's probably the type that won't speak,

But it was wrong of me to be so absurd,

Because she spoke and it made me feel weak.

She was smooth as silk as she sat in the chair,

No hurry, no worry it seemed,

So sweet, So complete with her long black hair,

Could this woman be made just for me.

I talked, she talked, we had no plans,

She really completes my day,

But I can't leave it as it stands,

I'll see her again, There's a way.

I can still see that serious look,

As I recited some words from my mind,

Then all of a sudden a smile overtook,

And those brown eyes began to shine.

I somehow felt she heard what I said,

As if I tried to remember each line,

Though they were no longer in my mind,

But in the eyes of a Lady so Fine.

As she drove off, I felt the urge,

To follow where ever she'd go,

But I guess I didn't have the nerve,

Thought it better to take it slow.

I looked, I saw, I had to know,

This woman who moved with such grace,

With luxurious hair all a glow,

And to top this a beautiful face.

Should I or shouldn't I, the question came,

I had to make up my mind,

I may not have this chance again,

So I'd better not waste any time.

I asked for her name, which she gave,

And in turn I gladly gave mine,

The sweet sound of her voice made me a slave,

Command me, I'm yours any time.

SWEET INSPIRATION

You're inspiring me, putting a fire in me,

Even though you're not trying,

A powerful explosion of ecstasy,

The whole truth and I'm, not lying.

With eyes that hold the key to love,

Shades of brown so unique;

I asked myself if there ever was,

Anyone in my lifetime as sweet.

That answer didn't take long to come,

I knew it all the while,

When my heart started beating like a drum,

As I gazed upon your lovely smile.

I don't feel we've met before,

But, I'm sure we ought to be,

Seeing each other a little more,

Because I sense a Love so sweet.

I'm, spellbound by your conversation,

And I'm mystified by your soft smile;

I'm positive this is no revelation,

LADY I like your style.

You've moved me more in a moments time,

Than I've been shook all year,

Pardon me, but, I wish you were mine,

In laughter and in tear.

I feel you need someone to Love you,

Someone who'll treat you right,

That someone who loves you true,

To console you through the night.

My search for Love could end right here,

And a new day could surely begin,

Just being Loved by you "My Dear"'

I could but only win.

And keeping that fire and desire burning,

Warming your heart, body, and mind,

Being near when you get a yearning,

And always reserving some time.

If opportunity knocks I'll be there,

And I won't be one who hesitates,

Making you aware of my Love and Care,

At the right time and right place.

So…just think of me a little each day,

Cause I'm certainly gonna be thinking of you,

And in time you might feel this way,

I'll be truly hoping you do.

"I STILL TREMBLE"

I still tremble, each time we meet,
Well, just about the same,
That tender voice that sounds so sweet,
When you call out my name.

Each time we talk on the phone,
I'm wishing you were here,
Then I'd have you here to myself alone,
So I could hold you near.

Sometimes I feel so out of place,
When there's nothing left to do,
So I just visualize your face,
With a passion just for you.

Expressing just the way I feel,
From the bottom of this heart,
And if this Love is really real,
Then we won't ever part.

Now when I say I Love You,

Don't think that I'm insane,

A little bit crazy, Yeh! Over you,

So I say it again and again.

I want a Love a real Love,

Not something that may resemble,

cause when it's you I think of…

All over again, I Tremble.

"DISTANT ONE"

Let me touch your wonderful Love,
I want to feel that magic moment,
You're everything that I've dreamed of,
Let's make both our hearts content.

Thinking of you in the early light,
Sometimes it gets hard to concentrate,
Dreaming of you all through the night,
Baby are you making me wait?

Let me hold you close to me,
As if there were no tomorrow,
I want to be the best I can,
Without any heartache or sorrow.

Touch me, when you feel the need,
Because I'll be there for you;
Just close your eyes and reach for me,
Love You? My Love I do.

Won't you let me touch your mind?
So I can sense where you want to go,
Then I'll be ready everytime;
All you need do is show.

The feelings I have are oh so deep,
You've got the Love I must have,
Although dreaming of you helps me sleep,
I want you here in my arms so bad.

You're that glow that star in my eyes,
I'm reaching to touch you're not there,
And when we're together time really flies,
Let me show you love, that I care.

Let me kiss your lips so tender,
with a taste like I've never known,
And I will give you sweet surrender,
with true Love that lasts on and on.

The thought of you makes my heart pound,

It's double time when it's you I'm gonna see,

But when I know you won't be around,

It gets to the best part of me.

Keep me in touch with your sweet Love,

The sound of your voice would suit me fine,

And in turn I'll give you a buzz,

To find out what's on your mind.

There is no reason why we should be distant,

When we have just only begun,

If you called I'd be there in a instant,

Be it riding or driving, I'd run.

Well…I'll be thinking of you,

And your wonderful touch,

I'll be dreaming of you too,

Because you mean …so very much.

Kelvin Brown

<u>TOTAL RECALL</u>

I STILL RECALL THE TIME
WHEN YOU WERE MINE
AND A SONG PLAYED IN MY HEART.

THE JOY THAT YOU'D BRING
MEANT ONLY ONE THING
I LOVED YOU FROM THE START.

THE NIGHTS SPENT TOGETHER
WE DIDN'T CARE WHETHER
WHO KNEW OR WHAT THEY MIGHT SAY.

WITH YOU IN MY ARMS
AFRAID OF NO HARMS
COULDN'T WAIT FOR THE NEWCOMING DAY.

THE TIME WASN'T FAR
YOU'RE STILL MY SWEET STAR
NO MATTER WHAT CHANGES MIGHT DO.

MY LOVE FLOWS ON FREE

THOUGH YOU'RE NOT WITH ME

CAN'T HELP BUT TO KEEP LOVING YOU.

TEARS FLOW UNDER MY CHIN

THAT'S JUST HOW ITS BEEN

WHEN I CAN'T HAVE YOU TO HOLD.

SHOULD A GROWN MAN CRY

WHEN HE FEELS JUST AS I

I'M LEFT ALL ALONE IN THE COLD?

THE MUSIC HAS HALTED

COULD I HAVE DEFAULTED

MY SENSES HAVE LOST THERE DIRECTION.

I'M LOVE SICK AND BLINDED

I'VE BECOME ABSENT MINDED

DESPERATE FOR YOUR SWEET AFFECTION.

NO, THIS CAN'T BE RIGHT

I CAN'T SLEEP AT NIGHT

I'M SO VERY TIRED IN THE MORNING.

THERE WAS NO SIGN

THAT YOU COULDN'T BE MINE

I WAS SHOCKED WITHOUT ANY WARNING.

A STRANGE THING OCCURRED

WITHOUT A MUTTERING WORD

"WE'RE THROUGH" NOW WHO TOLD YOU?

LIKE A THIEF IN THE NIGHT

YOU UPSET MY LIFE

NOT KNOWING JUST WHAT TO DO.

MY HEART'S IN THE DARK

MY SOUL HAS NO SPARK

I WANT YOU AND NOBODY ELSE.

I'VE TRIED ONE OR TWICE
BUT IT DIDN'T WORK RIGHT
WITHOUT YOU I'M NO LONGER MYSELF.

SHOULD I WAIT FOR THAT DAY
WHEN YOU COME BACK MY WAY
OR PLAY THE FIELD NOT FOR KEEPS?

THAT CAN'T BE THE WAY
I DON'T CARE WHAT THEY SAY
WITHOUT YOU IT'S SO HARD TO SLEEP.

I SAY NIGHTLY PRAYERS
AT THE TOP OF THE STAIRS
AS I GAZE UP TOWARD, THE SKY.

I'M SURE IT'S TAKEN
THAT WHEN I AWAKEN
THERE WILL BE YOU AND I.

WHEN I OPEN MY EYES
HOPE YOU'RE THE SURPRISE
THAT I HAVE BEEN LONGING TO HOLD.

IF I TREATED YOU TENDER

WOULD YOUR LOVE SURRENDER

DARLING, PLEASE DON'T MAKE ME FEEL COLD.

I WANT YOU, I NEED YOU

I'LL TRY HARD TO PLEASE YOU

DON'T TAKE YOUR SWEET LOVE AWAY.

I'VE GOT THE DESIRE

AND A VERY HOT FIRE

TO SHOW YOU IF YOU'D ONLY STAY.

KISS ME SOFT IN THE NIGHT

YOU DO IT JUST RIGHT

TAKE ME TO THE PROMISED LAND.

AND I'LL DO MY BEST

TO HANDLE THE REST

DOING MY PART AS YOUR MAN.

PLEASE PROMISE ME, LOVE
YOU'LL ALWAYS THINK OF
THE FEELINGS I TELL YOU ABOUT.

AND I'LL DO THE SAME
WHEN I CALL OUT YOUR NAME
IT SOUNDS SO SWEET I COULD SHOUT.

BUT YOUR LOVE IS SO GREAT
IT'S SAD IN THE WAIT
NEEDING YOUR SWEET GENTLE TOUCH.

IT'S FOR LOVE OF YOU
I DO WHAT I DO
I HUNGER FOR YOU SO MUCH.

HOPING YOU WANT FORGET
THAT MOMENT WE MET
WHEN SMILES WERE ON OUR FACES.

INSTEAD OF FALSE HOPES
HANDS TIED UP IN ROPES
AND THERE WAS NO ROOM FOR SPACES.

BRING YOUR LOVE BACK TO ME
OUR LOVE SHOULD FLOW FREE
I BELONG INSIDE OF YOU.

SO UNTIL YOU RETURN
MY HEART WILL STILL YEARN
FOR THE ONLY LOVE, I EVER KNEW.

TEARS OF JOY

When I made Love to you the first time,

It was a very astonishing surprise,

Thought I was about to lose my mind,

Then tears began falling from my eyes.

They were tears of joy and ECSTASY,

A feeling too intense to measure,

At that moment I was high as could be,

Like a miner just finding sought treasure.

I wanted it all, though It wasn't mine,

But oh how nice it would be,

I know you'll be gone in a matter of time,

Leaving me here helplessly.

If heavens like this, I've got to go,

How could there be something I missed?

Is this Heaven I've got to know?

You've got something I can't resist.

I don't need a high like other folk,

When it feels so good inside you,

You make me feel right, that's no joke,

You let your "Lovelight" shine through.

You soothe me, you groove me in every way,

I'm speechless, I'm spellbound, I'm mythed,

And I'm praying and hoping that you'll stay,

I'll make it worth while to be with.

The thought that you'd go hurts me so,

It's strange but I feel like sighing,

So while you're here please take it slow,

Although I just might start crying.

Where have you been my sensuous one,

The ingredient that I've been missing,

Don't let it end! We've just begun,

I want more and more of your kissing.

Now we've made Love a time or two,

And it's greater than ever before,

I feel as though I'm a part of you,

And my mind continues to soar.

To keep you, I will always be trying,

Because I do need you so,

I hope that you can get use to my crying,

But you take me where I want to go.

"CONSIDERATION"

I haven't had a real chance,
To let you know what's cooking,
I'd like to start a sweet romance,
Since you, I've stopped looking.

The few times that I've seen you,
I've watched your every move,
There's something about the way you do,
That puts me in a groove.

I know that you don't know me,
But, right now I wished you did,
For, I am thinking seriously,
That this just might be it.

Now I don't rap to every girl,
Or every lady that I meet,
So if you let me share your world,
I'd love you eternally.

Once you've known me for a while,

I'm sure you'll find me right,

Then show me, by your sweetest smile,

When I'm holding you tight.

I'll do for you to satisfy,

Your almost every whim,

And promise not to tell a lie,

Or, my name isn't Jim.

So, until we both might meet,

And, if that time may come,

I hope that you'll consider thoroughly,

And let me be the one.

STAR LOVE

Glimmering, shimmering, beautiful star,

You're as lovely as a ray of sun,

And by far you are a Quasar,

And you're twenty-four hours as one.

Day in, day out you have that glow,

Which touches this heart of mine,

Let me make you aware, so you'll know,

That you make my day just shine.

More brilliant as each day goes past,

A consistent thought in my brain,

With a vision of you that seems to last,

Until I see you again.

I never knew beauty could exist,

In a single heavenly form,

But now I know that this is it,

A woman so gentle, so warm.

If I could place you in a frame,

With that smile kept just for me,

I'd probably feel guilty and ashamed,

Keeping you from the world to see.

So I'd rather you have your beauty show,

For those who smell the roses,

And for the others, they know where to go,

When they turn up their snobby noses.

Well, let's skip all that, you're where it's at,

If you get any finer I'll scream,

It's not a theory it's a natural fact,

You're a Queen if you know what I mean.

That day I gazed at your sparkling ways,

Unaware of the beauty I'd see,

Putting my mine in a kind of a haze,

And so glad that you came to be.

Kelvin Brown

Even though you're not mine, I still think you're fine,

And I've said what I feel, I had,

And I'd say it again time after time,

You're incredibly lucious and "BAD"!

"TOUCH ME, SEE ME"

Can you see the years in my eyes?
The hurt and the sorrow I've felt?
Can you see the tears in my eyes?
My heart had turned cold, wouldn't melt.

Can you see the cracks in my smile?
There was no reason to laugh,
It took such a very long while,
thought it something I couldn't have.

Can you feel the past years pain?
Which make me stronger with time,
It leaves but then comes back again:
They have a space in my mind.

Touch the heart of a sensitive man,
who's known hate, but most of all Love,
In need of someone to understand;
With exception to the man from above.

75

See the mind of turning wheels;
Spinning in the most every direction,
See it, touch it, see how it feels,
to search for Love and affection.

Touch the soul of a man still learning;
that true Love is so hard to find,
touch the blood of a heart still churning,
From when true love was once mine.

For once in my life I touched someone,
whom I thought would last forever,
with face all a glow like a morning sun,
I'll Love her until time gets better.

She touched me in places, I wasn't aware,
she spoke words so soft and gently,
the combination would raise my hair,
Satisfying me physically and mentally.

For that, she's inherited all my Love,

A promise I gave til forever,

and as long as there's a sky above,

In my heart we'll always be together.

<u>PILLOW TALK</u>

The other night you gave me Pillow talk,

And it did something strange to me,

Without my car I started to walk,

To Fifty Seventh Street.

I know to you it might sound funny,

But to me it was hardly a joke,

I felt real weird in my "tummy"

and lighting smoke after smoke after smoke.

Why do you do me this way?

When it's so hard for me to bear,

You won't even give me a day,

just to show you that I care.

It's not that I don't like it,

Because you know I do,

It's just, I get so excited,

When the pillow talk comes from you.

I'd so much like to hold you tight,

And hear those words real clear,

At the time you think it's right,

So sweetly in my ear.

For now I can only dream,

And hope one day you might find,

Just how sweet and beautiful it could be,

Although it's only a matter of time.

I only want to really make it,

With a woman as fine as you,

I want a Love, got no time to fake it,

Let me prove that I'll be true.

Cuddle up real close to me,

And relax your body and mind,

Let us begin this special ecstasy,

That surpasses any other time.

Let me whisper words of passion,

The words to make you feel so warm,

It's not much that I'm asking,

Come fill these needing arms.

Just open up your heart to me,

And give me half a chance,

Let me show how good it could be,

With a true-to-life romance.

I feel for you so greatly,

More than you even know,

It didn't just happen lately,

I've always loved you so.

I will be so sweet to you,

I'll remind you how I feel,

And do the things you want to do,

To show my Love is Real.

So take the time to summarize,

Each word that I have said,

I hope that you will realize,

They're from my Heart and Head.

WONDERFUL WONDERFUL

It was a wonderful night,

Everything was so right,

passion was at it's Zenith.

Was the ultimate pleasure,

Too intense to measure,

With who, we wanted to be with.

In each other's eyes,

we found our surprise,

The one that we prayed and hoped for.

In each other's arms,

We felt each ones charms,

And preceded to want more and more.

The feelings I felt,

Would make any man melt,

Just to know, that one had the chance.

Such a gorgeous young lady,

Who drives me crazy,

With her sweet face full of romance.

And the tender soft skin,

That this woman came in,

Had this bright and sensuous glow.

As we lay in the dark,

I could hear but one heart,

I promised her that I'd take it slow.

And as sure as expected,

Our Love was connected,

So good, so real, so right.

It was more than an evening,

It was much more than pleasing,

This is one Hell of a night.

I pinched myself to make sure or not,

Confirmed, I know what I've got!

And these chosen moments won't be wasted.

Kelvin Brown

I'm going to give the best of me,

My all to build an ecstasy.

I want it so bad I can taste it.

Love as if there is no tomorrow,

If there's no sorrow,

I'm here with you to be one.

The feeling's we get,

Get's more powerful yet,

who cares if there's never a Sun?

You fit like a glove,

When we're making Love,

I wish I could stay so much longer.

But you make me so weak,

That I can but sleep,

Tomorrow I'm going to be stronger.

I'll always remember those special nights,

When we shared under staring lights,

The thoughts bring you back to me.

I can't help but remember,

Kissing lips so darn tender,

you take me to ecstasy.

I'll keep on loving you dear,

Whether you're far or near,

Your Loving remains in my heart.

It's safe here within,

Until all else ends,

As I promised my Love from the start.

<u>FOREVER HERE FOR YOU</u>

I can feel your breath upon my face,
As I lay here half-asleep.
I hope you like me in this space,
Hope I am the love you keep.

You sound as if you're humming
Our favorite old love song;
Now is there a heartbreak coming,
Or is our love still strong?

You've placed your hand upon my chest,
Oh so ever lightly;
Is this part of a little test,
Or do you want to excite me?

You've begun blowing in my ear,
You don't have to say a word;
Just come a little closer dear,
Because, I know what I heard.

You're telling me you love me,
So why would I question that?
You give your love so tenderly,
And I interact.

I needn't want for tenderness,
Or wonder if love is real;
I have it all and your loveliness,
It's the way you make me feel.

I can feel your lips upon my face,
As I lay here wide awake.
Now I know I have a place,
That no one else can take.

Now I think it's about time,
To stretch and hold you tight,
To let you know I am glad you're mine,
And to love you with all my might.

Kiss those lips so ever sweetly,

Just as long as you want me to,

And my darling I'll always be,

Forever here for you.

<u>MISS OR MRS.</u>

HELLO; MS. OR MRS.
WHATEVER THE CASE MAY BE,
I BELIEVE IN GRANTED WISHES;
I BELIEVE THAT YOU'RE FOR ME,

PLEASE…LET ME FINISH LET ME START,
TO TELL YOU JUST HOW I KNOW;
I CAN FEEL IT DEEP INSIDE MY HEART,
AND YOUR FACE IS ALL A GLOW.

I'LL NEVER PASS THIS WAY AGAIN,
SO WON'T YOU HEAR ME PLEASE;
I'LL MAKE IT SIMPLE AND PLAIN,
JUST OPEN YOUR HEART TO ME.

IF I STUTTER, WHEN I SPEAK,
ALLOW ME TO SLOW MY WORDS DOWN;
IT'S ONLY BECAUSE YOU MAKE ME WEAK,
WITH THE THOUGHT OF YOU BEING AROUND,

YOU'RE SO VERY BEAUTIFUL TO ME,

I DON'T WANT YOU TO GET AWAY,

I WANT TO LOVE YOU TOTALLY;

MY LOVE WANT GO ASTRAY.

I'M HOPING, PRAYING AND WISHING,

THAT YOU'LL TRY MY LOVE ONE TIME;

AND WE'LL FIND WHAT WE'VE BEEN MISSING,

AND FINALLY YOU'LL BE MINE.

I'LL GIVE YOU THE NEEDED ATTENTION,

LET YOU KNOW HOW MUCH I CARE,

AND BY THE WAY DID I MENTION?

I'LL LOVE YOU EVERYWHERE.

I'M GOING TO GIVE YOU ALL OF ME,

TO LOVE YOU ALL THE WHILE,

BE THE BEST MAN I CAN BE,

TO KEEP YOU IN THAT SMILE.

I'VE DONE MY TIME SEARCHING,

AND I HOPE IT ENDS RIGHT HERE;

I'M GOING TO SPEND MY TIME WORKING,

ON KEEPING YOU PLEASED MY DEAR.

THIS FEELING'S GOT ME GOING,

I'M SURE YOU'LL FEEL IT TOO,

I CAN TELL WE'LL BE ENJOYING;

A LOVE FOREVER NEW.

SO, TAKE MY HAND AND WE'LL GO THERE,

TO WHERE WE NEED TO BE;

I'LL GIVE YOU TENDER LOVING CARE,

WHILE YOUR LOVE FLOWS GENTLE AND FREE.

I KNOW THAT YOU'VE JUST MET ME,

AND THIS MAY COME AS A SHOCK;

BUT, I DON'T WANT YOU TO FORGET ME,

CAUSE MY LOVE WON'T EVER STOP.

SO AGAIN MISS OR MRS.
PLEASE TELL ME YOUR NAME;
I KNOW, I'M A LITTLE AMBITIOUS,
AND MAYBE IN TAD INSANE.

BUT, MY TOMORROW COULD DEPEND ON YOU,
OUR LIVES WOULD BE SO RIGHT,
I'VE HAVE YOU TO HOLD ON TO,
AND YOU WOULD BY MY WIFE.

I'M GOING TO ASK YOU ONCE AGAIN,
I'M GIVING IT ALL I'VE GOT;
I WANT YOU SO, I FEEL LOVE PAINS,
IT DOESN'T MATTER IF YOU'RE MARRIED OR NOT.

I NEED TO HAVE YOU IN MY LIFE,
I DON'T WANT TO EXIST WITHOUT YOU;
I WANT YOU EVERY DAY AND NIGHT,
I'LL PAINT YOUR GRAY SKIES BLUE.

<u>JUST ANOTHER HOLIDAY</u>

It's just another holiday,
To remind myself of you;
Of how we use to laugh and play,
And love the whole night through.

It won't be like it use to be,
With all that Christmas cheer,
And I won't have a nice pine tree,
Or ever hold you near.

I don't feel like having fun,
And my thoughts are not on singing,
My shopping list consists of only one;
Which I know, Santa won't be bringing.

The music doesn't help me much,
They play it all night long;
A mistletoe a tender touch,
A where did I go wrong.

93

And not forgotten that firm embrace,
And that soft smooth skin aglow;
Those rosy cheeks upon your face,
Being touched by the falling snow.

I've never seen smiles so bright,
Than the ones you showed to me;
And how they brightened up my life,
As sweet as they could be.

It's just another holiday,
Guess I shouldn't feel too bad;
To have loved, to have felt that way,
Should at least make my heart glad.

For reasons I can't help myself,
I'm feeling a little bit down,
It's hard for me to love someone else,
Even though she's not around.

I thought by now I'd be fine,

To love somebody new,

But she's always on my mind;

Then I become a little bit blue.

I don't regret to love those days,

I'd do them once again;

But if the lover you must take away,

At least leave me the friend.

So it's just another holiday,

And this love should be winding down,

Then I can love a brand new way,

With someone who's ...Around.

<u>STAY</u>

You've given me joy for quite some time,
And I still feel it all the while,
It's so very hard to picture in my mind,
Being without your sweet smile.

We've been doing a lot of changing,
At times, I don't know what to do,
If we could start some rearranging,
Maybe we could start our love anew.

I'm just not ready to give up now,
We've had our good times and bad,
Why don't we try to figure out how,
We can again make the good times last.

I believe that you still love me,
I can feel it deep down in my heart,
An heaven forbid us, if we…
Should ever, ever part.

Let's give it one more chance,

Let's do it right this time,

Let's get it together and make some plans,

I want you forever as mine.

If you have faith, believe I can,

Trust in what I do and say,

Let me be your one and only man,

And we can go all the way.

Give me back the tender smile,

Share with me that joy you bring,

And I'll reveal the kind of style,

That makes you sing.

I've missed the love we once shared,

And sweet kisses so tenderly,

I miss the times when we both cared,

When you and I were "we".

Just find it deep inside of you,
The feelings that you hold dear,
There you'll discover a love that's true,
Where ever, when ever, we're near.

Come be with me, let's work it out,
Don't you think that it's about time?
You're the one I need without a doubt,
I hope and pray that you'll stay as mine,

<u>NIGHT AND DAY</u>

COMING INTO MY LIFE WAS EASY,

BECAUSE I'D BEEN WAITING ALL ALONG;

YOU CAME THERE TO PLEASE ME,

AND HOW MY HEART WOULD BEAT STRONG.

A SMILE SO SWEET AND SENSUOUS,

AND LIPS THAT WOULD MAKE ME MELT;

AS WE HELD EACH OTHER, SO RIGHT FOR US,

TOUCHING FEELINGS THAT HAD NEVER BEEN FELT.

YOU SHOWED YOUR BEAUTIFUL GLOW TO ME,

THROUGH MORE WAYS THAN ONE,

AND I NEVER KNEW LOVE COULD BE,

AS WARM AS THE MORNING SUN.

I WAS READY TO GO TO ANY LENGTH,

AS LONG AS I WOULD END UP WITH YOU,

I KNEW MY HEART HAD THE STRENGTH,

TO LOVE YOU AND ALWAYS BE TRUE.

YOU SHOWED ME THAT DREAMS COULD BE,
IF YOU REALLY TRUSTED YOUR HEART;
THE SWEETEST PART OF REALITY,
AND A SPECIAL KIND OF ART.

YOU WERE THAT DREAM AND EVERYTHING,
THAT MEANT THE WORLD TO ME;
BUT NOW I'M JUST RECOVERING,
FROM THAT WHICH CAN NO LONGER BE.

YOU SAID THE LOVE YOU HAD TO SHARE,
WASN'T HALF AS STRONG AS MINE;
SAID YOU TRIED BUT, IT WASN'T THERE,
AND IT WAS JUST A WASTE OF TIME.

AT THAT MOMENT, MY HEART STOOD STILL,
AND I SEEMED TO HAD LOST MY BREATH;
DIDN'T KNOW HOW TO REACT, HOW TO FEEL,
LIKE A MAN BEING SENTENCED TO DEATH.

I DIDN'T HAVE TIME TO BRACE MYSELF,
I DIDN'T EVEN SEE IT COMING;
BUT I KNEW I HAD TO FACE MYSELF,
AND IT DIDN'T MAKE SENSE TO START RUNNING.

THERE WAS NO CURE TO MAKE ME BETTER,
THE WORDS, THEY CLUNG TO MY MIND,
ALTHOUGH SHE PREFERRED TO WRITE A LETTER,
AND WELL…THAT JUST SUITS ME FINE.

MY HEART CONTINUES TO LOVE HER SO,
AND MY HEAD WITHSTANDS THE PAIN;
MY LOVE KEEPS DRIVING, I CAN'T LET GO,
AND, I'D DO IT ALL OVER AGAIN.

FOOLS RUSH IN…I STAND ACCUSED,
THIS IS THE PRICE I PAY,
ALTHOUGH I FEEL A BIT MISUSED,
I STILL LOVE HER NIGHT AND DAY.

Kelvin Brown

<u>NATURALLY DESIGNED</u>

I LOOKED, I SAW, I HAD TO KNOW,
THIS WOMAN WHO MOVED WITH SUCH GRACE,
WITH LUXURIOUS HAIR ALL A GLOW,
AND TO TOP THIS A BEAUTIFUL FACE.

SHOULD I OR SHOULDN'T I THE QUESTION CAME,
I HAD TO MAKE UP MY MIND,
I MAY NOT HAVE THIS CHANCE AGAIN,
SO I'D BETTER NOT WASTE ANY TIME.

I ASKED FOR HER NAME, WHICH SHE GAVE,
AND IN TURN I GLADLY GAVE MINE,
THE SWEET SOUND OF HER VOICE MADE ME A
SLAVE,
COMMAND ME, I'M YOURS ANYTIME.

THIS LADY HAD MOVES STANDING STILL,
HER BODY HAD SOFT DEFINITION,
JUST HER PRESENCE GAVE ME A THRILL,
SO I DARE NOT THINK OF HER KISSIN.

WE TALKED FOR A WHILE AS WE SAT,
SAID SHE'D LIVED HERE FOR A SHORT TIME,
AND WHERE SHE WAS FROM, SHE'S GOING BACK,
NOW, THIS IS ABUSE TO MY HEART AND MIND.

BUT WHAT CAN I SAY, IT HAPPENS THAT WAY,
WHEN I FIND SOMEONE SO APPEALING,
I WISH SOMEHOW I COULD MAKE HER STAY,
WELL, I GUESS I SHOULD CANCEL THAT FEELING.

IT'S SO NICE TO KNOW BEAUTY'S OUT THERE,
PHYSICALLY AND MENTALLY COMBINED,
WITH A CARING HEART, WHICH IS SO RARE,
IN WOMEN SO NATURALLY DESIGNED.

IF YOU CAME BACK TOMORROW

If you arrive at lights morning,
With hopes that you'd only stay,
Without hesitation, without warning,
I'd love as if you were never away.

If you came to me at midnight,
I'd welcome you with open arms,
You'll forever be that sweet delight,
With your special delectable charms.

I couldn't imagine refusing you,
We go back a long, long, road,
Whatever it was, confusing you,
I hope your life has slowed.

Where you've been, I won't question,
As long as you're here with me,
But I'd like to make a suggestion,
Would you, could you make it eternally?

I've love so long and deeply,

I need this love we've built,

And I won't let it fail so easily,

And I won't let it wilt.

It'll take more than high winds,

Or thunderstorms and rains,

Because my love weaves and bends,

When it's all been done, my love remains.

If you came home this evening,

I'd shower you with love and laughter,

I'd make it an evening of pleasing,

And you'd be consumed by the rapture.

Whenever you came back home,

I just want to touch your face,

Because right now I'm so alone,

And my love shouldn't go to waste.

Kelvin Brown

Just come to me whenever you can,

Anyway, anytime, anyhow,

What would make me a happy man?

If you could come right now.

<u>UNFADED LOVE</u>

Heavens no, my love hasn't faded!
Not simply because you're gone,
As a matter of face it's been upgraded,
My love grows on and on.

Although you're physical presence,
Is not where I can really touch,
I can still feel the essence,
You have left me with that much.

I can see that smile you wore,
From that very last sighting,
And feel that passion to the core,
From your very last writing.

I think about you even now,
There's always room and space,
It's not hard, I just know how,
You have a special place.

I find myself attempting to resist,

Thinking about you this way,

I hope to you, I still exist,

Since that bittersweet day.

Every now and then I see a likeness,

And my heart beats like a drum,

Then my mind begins to fight this,

Because it's just not the original one.

Apparently, I don't have the sense,

To give up on your sweet love,

Merely thinking of you and I'm intense,

Than I never ever was.

I maybe should have stopped loving you,

At least a year or two later,

But the thought of someone hugging you,

Only makes my love greater.

I know it seems a waste of time,

With a love so strong and bold,

Someday I might just lose my mind,

Or wind up alone and old.

If I didn't know any better,

I could swear you feel my vibes,

But I just can't decide whether,

To live two separate lives.

I'm sure you think about me,

If but only time to time,

I will continue to love you eternally,

From day one, you've been mine.

FREE MY LOVE

I can't go on, too much longer,
I must have my freedom to love,
I am trying my best to be stronger,
I've asked every star up above.

What did you ever do to me?
That I wasn't feeling aware,
To make me crave so intensely,
And that fills me with a scare.

I've tried so hard to break away,
Even moved to a brand new place,
I tried to start a brand new day,
But every where I see your face.

I toss and turn till morning light,
I'm awake till almost then,
I only get weaker when I fight,
It doesn't seem like it's going to end.

It isn't making any sense,

Why you'd do such a thing to me,

Make me love you with false intent,

And leave me just to be.

I wonder if it is a spell,

That keeps my mind on you,

It's beginning to feel like hell,

When only loving you will do.

I want my love, as before,

To give love as I will,

Instead you leave this open door,

That decides I'm not to feel.

To love you and no one else,

You're having the time of your life,

And I'm here all by myself,

And you've become a new wife.

Did you forget to lift the spell?

That you have cast on me?

Then free me from this living hell,

Let me go set my love free.

Was it something in the food I ate?

Or was it something in my drink?

This kind of love, I hate,

It's controlling the way I think.

If only you could come back here,

To undo what you have done,

And make these feelings disappear,

So that I might love someone.

I would do the same for you,

Won't you please have a heart?

I don't deserve to live life blue,

Return my emotional part.

Maybe one day you'll hear my cry,

Just maybe in the nick of time,

And allow my love to soar, to fly,

And to beam like fresh sunshine.

Release me …. Please

PLEASURATION

PLEASURATION IS GIVING LOVE, DEVOTION, ATTENTION, CARING, SHARING, TIME AND ALL THOSE GOOD THINGS TO YOUR MATE, TO THE EXTENT THAT, THERE IS NO NEED OUTSIDE PERSUASIONS.

PLEASURATION IS FOCUSING SOLELY ON THAT MATE. LEARNING DAILY JUST HOW TO FULFILL THE DESIRED NEEDS AND WHEN TO ACT AND INTERACT ON SPECIFIC EMOTIONS.

PLEASURATION IS SOMETIMES ASKING YOUR SELF QUESTIONS SUCH AS: WHAT WOULD IT BE LIKE WITHOUT MY LOVE? COULD I GET ON WITH MY LIFE, WITHOUT MY LOVE? IS THERE SOMEONE OUT THERE I MIGHT CONSIDER HAVING BESIDES MY MATE? AND IF SO, IS IT ACTUALLY WORTH LEAVING MY LOVE FOR SOMEONE ELSE? AFTER ASKING THESE QUESTIONS AND COMING TO YOUR CONCLUSIONS, THERE'S A GOOD CHANCE YOU'LL KEEP YOUR RELATIONSHIP GOING ON STRONGER, THIS IS PART OF PLEASURATION.

PLEASURATION IS KEEPING YOUR RELATIONSHIP NEW AND ALIVE AND WELL. OCCASIONALLY BEING

SPONTANEOUS IN AREAS WHERE YOU HAVEN'T BEEN, OR PROMPTLY INTERACTING WHEN YOUR MATE BECOMES SPONTANEOUS. FEELING GOOD ABOUT CHANGE...THAT'S PLEASURATION.

PLEASURATION IS OPENING THE DOOR LIKE YOU DID WHEN YOU FIRST MET, GIVING YOUR MATE THAT FEELING THAT YOUR FEELINGS ARE STILL JUST AS STRONG.

BUT MOST OF ALL...PLEASURATION IS WHAT YOU BELIEVE THAT YOU NEED TO DO, TO HAVE A MEANINGFUL AND LASTING RELATIONSHIP WITH YOUR MATE.

ABOUT THE AUTHOR

I'm Kelvin Brown, born in Chicago, Illinois. I grew up in a little south suburban town called Robbins, Illinois (Now residing in Kenosha, Wisconsin). I attended schools in Robbins, Illinois and surrounding areas (Oaklawn and Midlothian).

I'm the third born of six sisters and two brothers and a wonderful Father and Mother. I have two sons Kelvin Brown Jr. and Kendall Lewis Brown.

Since the age of ten, I've been able to put words and phrases together, in a way that created a feeling. After years of writing, I decided that it was time to share some of my works of poetry. I hope that you will be touched by… *Pleasuration.*

Sincerely,

Kelvin Brown

Made in the USA
Middletown, DE
16 July 2023

35238561R00076